Thought Fodder

Thought Fodder

Tom Heenan

Thought Fodder: Tom Heenan

Copyright © Tom Heenan 2020

First published 2020

All rights reserved. Without limiting the rights under copyright reserved above, no part of this publication may be reproduced, stored in or introduced into a database and retrieval system or transmitted in any form or by any means (electronic, mechanical, photocopying, recording or otherwise) without the prior written permission of both the owner of copyright and the above publishers.

Original illustrations: Tom Heenan

Cover design: Olivia Reid

ISBN: 978-0-6487555-0-0   Paperback
ISBN: 978-0-6487555-1-7   E-book

Thanks for helping, Liv.

Published with the assistance of angelkey.com.au

Window shoppers

Window shoppers, tyre kickers, ice cream lickers.
All the ones who won't buy,
just want to eat up your time.
Because they have it
and you don't.

Mm, that one looks OK.
Do you have it in red?
It's a bit small.
It's a bit big.
Do you think it will fit, hun?
Yeah, I dunno, did you measure?
No, I can guess.

Window shoppers, tyre kickers, ice cream lickers.
How much for that?
What can you do it for?
Is that your best price?
Does my bum look big in this?
Did you write it yourself, is this you playing?!

Window shoppers, tyre kickers, ice cream lickers.
Yeah, I'll ask the boss.
I've got the money next week.
Will you take a cheque?
All the ones who won't buy,
just want to eat up your time.
Because they have it
and you don't.

3 Large Men

340 kilograms
If they were one
The three large men

Single file past reception
Failing to stop the crying
And others from seeing

340 kilograms
If they were one

Embarrassed still

Mutual grief – a
dying sister and
life long friend

Single file past the
other rooms with
other dying sisters
and life long friends

They were 340 kilograms
If they were one
The three large men

Unable to stop the tears

Worthy

The best chance to most someones'
(no-ones or every ones)
of being someone is:
Your own death.
A death of some note.
Note worthy.
Notoriety for some.
Newspaper article worthy.
Facebook share worthy.
Fund raiser worthy.
Reddit worthy.
Insta worthy.
Could it be Rupert worthy?
Darwin Awards worthy?
Red carpet worthy.
Bio worthy.
Book worthy.
Heartfelt notices in the classifieds.
Classified worthy!
Worthy so very briefly.
Were you worthy?
To be noticed.
Dead.

                Doubt
           My God is Doubt
          I believe in Doubt
           My Doubt is Me
            I am My Belief
       My Belief is My God
          I Doubt My God

Case of the Missing Space

I looked and THE space wasn't there.
I know that the SPACE had been there.
A large space, recognisable ANY where,
as a space.

But now, WHERE the space
used to be
There WAS no space.

So, when do you think THAT
You first noticed that the SPACE
wasn't there?

Well I don't know,
You get so USED to seeing the space
Because it's always been there.
It is hard TO know
When I first noticed that
The space wasn't there
any more.

So you don't REMEMBER a time when
The space wasn't there
And that there was nothing
FILLING the space?

No, I don't think that I do.

Can you remember a time when THE SPACE was there?

I can, I sure can...
The space was there for sure..
I saw it all the time.
The space

Mind the   ☐ ☐ ☐

Fear

Do you remember? The fear.
There, in the wardrobe, big eyes leering out
from the coat-hangers.
And there, ducking down
behind the end of the bed.
And there, tapping at the window.
And you snatch your leg back under the sheet,
because you know it is reaching for that leg
hanging out of the bed.
Sweating hot in the face;
your eyes straining to make out
the shape in the darkness.

Mum, you quietly whisper yell.
And wait for a long long 10 seconds.
Mum, you whisper yell more loudly.

What's the matter?

Light storms the room making all of them invisible now.

I can't sleep. Hand on forehead.
You're hot, do you feel alright? A bit sick in the stomach.

You'll be ok. Good night. Mum? What?
If I die before I wake up will I know about it?
Don't be stupid, you're not going to die tonight.
What's it like mum? I don't know, we'll all find out one day.
Is it like sleeping? Yes, it's just like sleeping. Goodnight.
'Night Mum.

Good place

He was a mummy's boy
Back when that was a slag
40 years on he has changed

His mum is now a tiny thing
24-seven baby-care required

And we love each other
Don't we son, says mum
He said we sure do
Always have done

He was a mummy's boy
Back when that was a slag
90 years on she has changed

So, what happened last mum
I don't know
You don't remember
No, I don't

You dreamt of the dress to wear
to show that you were dead
And how your hair should be done
Make sure that you look good

Yes, that was it
My hair and the dress
And Jude

You want to see Jude
Yes I do
Do you know what that means
Well, I think so

Do you know where God is
Is God a place
Yes, he said, I think it is
Yes, me too, a Good place

One Goodbye

On a Wednesday afternoon
Holding hands or a hand
Long bony fingers
Not moving very much
Not much to say
At this point
Other than
I love you mum
"hnmnm"
This is one goodbye

Less

I started off knowing nothing
And now know less and less
And know now less
And now less
And less
And now
I know nothing

Mastering Zen

I was Mastering Zen
The other day
Looking, looking
Trying to see
The inner self
Beaming that 3rd Eye
Right at my navel
And further as well

A whole lot of gazing
It can get a bit blurry
There's no clarity there

3rd Eye, Right Eye, Minds' Eye
Fuck this
Close every eye
See it?
No, nothing
So open up and try
The Left Eye

Yeah nah that's right
The Left Eye's got it
It's the left eye

Mastering Zen

Mind the

On the Verge

I am on the verge of madness
It is difficult to believe
That I am here
Seeing these things

And I want to ask
Is this for real
What are you doing
And why

This awake dream is what
Temperature of 39.8 degrees
Has its say

I ask are you real
You touch my hair

I try to avoid it
But can't
Don't touch me

And then
I know
You are not real
Dead 10 years ago

An awake dream
Temperature of 39.8 degrees
I don't know how
I can see at all

I am on the edge of normal
It is difficult to believe
That I am here
Seeing these things

I say
This is real
What am I doing
And ask myself, why

I ask you, are you real
What are you doing
And why
I reach to touch your hair

You try to avoid it
But can't
Don't touch me

And I know
You are not real
Dead 10 years ago

This awake dream is a
Temperature of 39.8 degrees
Having its way

On the verge of madness
It is not a dream
I am doing this

And I have to say

Stop

Goodbyes

Greggy said once he only had a Jimi lick, a Mick Taylor riff
and a Keith riff. But I think that was false modesty.
He was pretty good.
In the end he got what he said he wanted,
which was not to get old. Fifty-two?

I waved goodbye to him from across the Vine bar,
we hadn't been talking for a few weeks.
3 hours later, he was dead.
And that was that.
They rang at the pub to tell me.

I waved goodbye to dad too, across two rooms
and through the music room doors.
Monday morning I'm off to Kerang ANZ for the week,
him for surgery at the Repat on Thursday.
Friday morning, he was dead.
And that was that.
They rang at the bank to tell me.

And at the exact time of Jude passing.
A pocket dial – if that was what did it –
the music on the answering machine
sounded like it was under water,
definitely a guitar.
And the so familiar voices,
sounding distorted and so far away.
A water warble version of Amazing Grace.
And that was that.
Jude rang at home to tell me…

Old?

He woke up and decided. Today, I am Old.

Why?

Age

An age – 80
Realising immortality is only in books
60 years wasted, trying

An age – 32
A feeling of overwhelming tiredness
Had this headache too long

An age – 53
An epiphany: fuck, not too long to go
And what, till then?

An age – 13
A bloody epiphany: well, this is fucked
What happens now?

An age – 65
Five years of agony
No way to stop it

An age – 1
Not knowing consciousness
Barely in the world

An age – 17
A coming, a quick one
No second one

An age – 1000
To be born again, sings Van
The Buddha and reincarnation

An age – any age
Knowing that I have this long left, a last year,
a last month, last day, hour, minute.
One second can be an age.

Age

Old Age?

The Girl on a Program

Too many options I said
Ah I'm looking for a particular brand
Earth Choice
I said yeah here's the washing one, the other stuff is...
Yeah, I'm in a program at the moment
A flat on my own
Is there a powder
Not by Earth Choice I didn't think
There's that one but it's expensive
Yeah nah I don't want that
Is this one ok for top loaders though,
I know that sounds dumb
No; yeah, it is ok for top loaders,
you don't know
until you find out, do ya
Thanks mate she said
Have a good day
Oh no worries
I don't know much
But I am interested

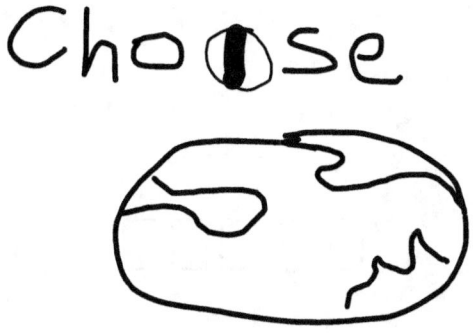

Tram #2

I am on a packed tram
Heading down Lygon Street
To meet Liv and Tom
For Japanese.

Norb and Elke at home
playing games on the TeeVee.
Sebastian wriggling in the pram,
having a sook.

It's the harsh voice,
"Hey ya dumb cunt,
shut the kid up."

I'm processing, What?
"It's a pram", I say, "I'm trying.
I'll fit it in here."

He's an old guy who's tough to start with but
weakness and resignation soon kick in.
He's in dirty white tracky daks,
on the back foot now, "Yeah, yeah, whatever."
Nobody else taking notice
or giving a fuck.

"I've got the pram.
I'm putting it here.
That's what the space is for."
I'm not saying it but in my head it's
Fuck You You Old Cunt.

Mind my seat   ☐☐☐ ☐☐☐

I will call him Large

Large was standing next to the parking meter,
he says, "c'mon what are you doing?",
almost nicely.
Large's driver was ferreting about,
says something
that wasn't heard.
He took the plunge and said
"fucking hurry up will ya?"
Stance on him like a basket-balling adult kid,
wearing a number 7 singlet.
Smoking a rolly.

She says "what did you say?"
He says "nothing, just c'mon", resigned to what's coming.
"Nooo, tell me what you just said ya fucken cunt,
I know you said somethin'
you fucken large cunt.
So fucken tell me
what you just said."

Large says - to me -
the only person walking past,
"whadda you know fucker."
Nah, I don't know much mate,
but I am interested.

And yeah, I heard what you said.

Tram #1

We are on the packed tram
heading up Bourke Street
to meet Suze and Norb
for Japanese.
Their sitters organised,
the catch up a long time coming.

It is the harsh voice,
"What are you looking at cunt?"
Violence and anger in a short question.
A young guy in the white trackies outfit,
on the back foot and shitting himself.
Everyone else backing out in a circle
as best they can.
"Ah nothing mate, I'm not looking at anything."
"Bull-fuck cunt, you're fucken looking at me."

Fuck I think, why now, and step through people,
three-deep looking in.
Everyone quiet.
"Hey mate, what's going on?"

Instant shift of attention,
"What the fuck its to you cunt."
"Ah I'm just wondering you know,
are you all right?"

"Phhhffff, fucking right, am I all right,
Yeah mate, I'm fucken all right, I'm just fucken great.
These cunts here fucken know, don't they."

"Yeah yeah, I don't think it's about you, you know"
"Oh yeah you reckon you know do ya."
"No, no, I'm not saying I know anything,
but I am interested."

A birthday gathering

Craig says, "Ah Will, the neighbour is sawing some branches on your side. He, um, seems a bit manic."

"Ah right, thanks", I say, stepping onto the back verandah. "Hey mate", I say, "what's going on?"

"Your fence there, it's falling over." He is chopping more than sawing branches of the paulownia. "And you put this top bit on the fence without telling us. Me lawyer says you've got 24 hours to take it down."

"No, come on mate, I don't think that's right."

"Yeah it's right. I'm angry too. I'm really angry. Someone called the cops on me."

"Well, it wasn't me."

"Bullshit, it wasn't you. You walked past Monday night and you never do that".

"No, come on, maybe someone was concerned for you."

"And then the cops were around half an hour later. And somebody dobbed me in for the rabbits before that. Nah, fuck you".

He chucks the saw and he's off through his carport.

"Mate it wasn't me", talking to the fence.
"I really want to talk to you about this."

I know he's heard me but he's just banging things about in the carport. I go back inside for a breather and a quick strong drink.

The chopping with the saw starts up again and he is throwing the branches into our yard. Vee says, "Don't go back out."
But I know I just have to.

"Hey mate, like I said, it wasn't me."

He stops sawing and calmer now says, "Yeah. Yeah, I thought about that. But someone fed the Jack Russell bits of glass. Had the vet bill to pay, a thousand bucks."

"Ah that is horrible, I didn't even know. I'm sorry to hear that."

"They told me to get a hobby. So I got the rabbits and then someone dobbed me in for that. The smell or the birds coming for the feed or something. So I put the corrugated iron around the carport".

"Man, that is really terrible, I'm sorry to hear all of that. You remember we had a dog, Hess, an Irish Terrier. That time we put your three little ones back over when they got under the fence? Well two anyway, we walked the old one back around to you. She was a bit sore."

"Oh yeah, yeah I do remember that".

"Mate, I'm sorry, I should know your name."

"Yeah, yeah it's Jim."

I get up to the fence, put my hand up and say, "I'm Will."

He said, "Yeah, yeah, I'm sorry. It's been really hard, the shit that's been happening. The missus is real sick too. And I've had a couple of beers. I know I shouldn't."

"Yeah, no, it's all right mate. Hey, how about I come around and have a look at that fence with you and we can have a chat. How about Tuesday?"

"Yeah, yep, that would be good. It's on an angle, you know. I didn't want it wrecking your olive tree."

"Yeah for sure, thanks for that. Tuesday, about 5 ok? And look, I don't know much but I am interested."

Kittens

I look up and she says
Hi, um, my friend Krys used to live here

Oh yeah, she did, on a program
Yeah, um, she left three kittens here
Oh did she now

Along with all the damage and the filth
and the rubbish everywhere

Four foot nine
Bold as brass

Um, yeah, I'm only concerned
About the kittens

Oh are you. Me, not so much

So, have you seen them
Ah no I haven't

Ok, um you know the gates
My dad put up for Krys
Could he come and get them back

There are many thoughts
going through my head right now
Hmm well I don't know
What's your dad's name
I'm stalling. Mick. Mick who
Mick Randolph

Right Mick Randolph
Ok yeah, if he can take the hinges off the posts as well
that would be good

Yeah ok, can he come any time
Yeah, sooner is better
And hey, where is Krys

Um, ah I'm not sure

Ah ok maybe, maybe she's with the kittens

The Two Car episode

The commodore pulls up quick
No rego plates front or back
A ford wagon, white too, pulls up right behind
#1 (passenger of commodore) gets out
Aggressively, very confident,
straight up to #2 (driver of ford)

#2 opens up the window
They know each other
Prince on the radio,
How can you just leave me standing...

Short convo
#2 starts rolling a ciggie
#1 gets on the mobile
#3 (driver of commodore) gets involved

#1 is pacing between the cars
In the ford there's at least two more baseball caps
with small bodies underneath in the back seat

#3 leans in to #2
Who is nodding quickly yes
#3 half jumps the bonnet, Starsky style
to squat beside the baseball caps
open back door and offer sage advice
Right outside the council office doors

#1 hangs up the mobile, dramatic like
Says something quick to
#3 and #2
He turns and quick strides it to
the commodore with #3 strutting behind

Jump in, a big ga-rumpff of the commodore and they're off
#1 says fuck the mobile, dramatic like
#3 agrees that that is bullshit

Decisions made and agreed or

Which space?

Physical
Mental
Structural
Energetic
Esoteric
Meta-physical
Aural
Existential
Wasted
Re-built
Personal
Multi-dimensional
Town
Country
Rural Residential
Zoned Commercial 1
(STCA)
Outback
Enclosed
Your
Missing
My

Space

Iris

He stalks the rooms, the house is a full 2000 metres squared.
Floors 15 by 10, clouds of sweet vape
leaving him ahead as he paces and talks.

Artworks set back on walls, the walking is quick
but measured, a designated path almost.
Close to the perimeters with all of the
artefacts lining the track.

Asking Iris, "why is no one here?"
Then, "take this down Iris",

"They listen but do not hear.
They hear but do not remember.
They remember but do not comprehend.
If they ever comprehend, they ignore. Stop."

The lights flicker, unnerving him.
He looks up to check the cameras
and the speakers and the lights.

Asking Iris, "why is no one here?"
Then, "Iris, take this down."

"They wanted to leave, they left.
Even after being told what was out there.
They listen but do not hear. Stop."

He's thinking, "Alone in the room with your thoughts.
Standing in a crowd alone, bored with the company,
that is you. But there is no crowd,"

would be good to fit in there somewhere.

"Iris, what are we waiting for?

Take this down. They hear but do not remember, comprehend but ignore. Stop."

To himself, "I asked for silence, please, just a little peace and quiet." I got it in spades.

The lights flicker again and he checks again the cameras and speakers and lights but is now confident the batteries will hold. Is there something missing somewhere?

To himself and the room, "Silence, please, just a little piece of quiet. They remember but do not comprehend.

Iris, why are we waiting?"

He stalks the rooms. Pacing is quick but measured, against the walls. Clouds of sweet vape leaving him ahead of Iris.

He says, "Iris, take this down. If they ever comprehend, they ignore"...

As Iris swings the heavy sword in an arc and from behind slices through him from right collar bone to left hip. He slumps to the floor in two parts, top half, then bottom.

And there is silence. Just a little peace and quiet.

And in Iris' mind, "why is no one here? Take this down, Iris. Stop".

And then

It was in a dream
Full moon minus a sliver
Grey white sky all you can see

And then
A perfect two humped camel
Moving from west to east
I can even see the basket
Moonlight shadows through wicker
Moon continues northward
The camel moves on east

And then
Comes a perfect blanket cloud
Light and airy and white; mostly all see-through
Gliding and clouding across the north moving moon

The camel has gone

And then
Jay was alive and well
Except he'd been dead
A little while now, I told Marty and Bruce
Who were surprised he was alive but
Not that he was doing well in property
Behind the new Rose Road

And then
It was a dream
A sliver of black on a full moon
Not a cloud to be seen
A city appears
House by house by apartment by building
by New York skyscraper

And then
There was a cloud in the dream
Nothing of the moon but a shining sliver
Grey white sky covering all you can see

My god

I'm walking past Pie Window, smelling pastry and meat delights. He is on the corner, standing on the garden bed stone wall, waving some paper and shouting,

"In the name of god we pray.
Because my gods are better than yours, yes they are."

Of course, I'm not that interested.

"In the name of god I say, you better believe.
Because mine is just, wise and good."

"So much more so than yours" he says, straight to me.

"In the name of god we pray, why can't we just be!?
Holy wars create holy hell for peace and heaven on earth."

They do go on. Self-righteous, talking to their own failings. And to me, ever so much in passing.

She is standing on the opposite corner garden bed stone wall. Waving brochures as she shouts,
"My god is better than your god, oh yes she is."
"So much more so than yours" she says, straight to me.

And then, as if in confidence and of utmost importance,
"Why limit yourself to one self when there are so many selfs to work together, with a common goal and good intention. This is my god. Better than yours."

My god. They do go on.

30 metres on, on a council seat outside the Reject Shop.
The dad is saying, "Look love, we didn't know it was gunna be like this." 10.30 Monday morning, he looks unhealthy
and out of it as well.
The mum is marching out of the Reject Shop.
"This is bullshit", she says, talking but not stopping.
"I'm gonna talk to someone about this", maybe heading for the bank in the mall but having to pass by the "My god is better than your god, you know" types, spruiking from the stone walls.

That could be fun to see but I won't go back to look.

The daughter is sitting next to the dad, looking straight down,
knees up, chin down and arms crossed.
Saying, "I haven't got any more money, dad."
He says, "I know love, we didn't think it was gunna be like
this. But it won't take long and we won't ask again."
She says, "But it hurts and you said them things last time".

And I turn into the Reject Shop as the woman spruiker
has come from the stone wall and is telling them,
"My god is better than your god, oh yes she is."

"Oh Jesus," I hear the dad say. And then the mum's coming
back, shouting this time, "Get away from there, you.
I told you before, this is bullshit, we don't need your crap."

They do go on.

He says, "I know it hurts love. I am sorry about that,
this time will be nice."

The mum is saying, don't you Billy Joel me.

I'm in the reject shop so I can't be sure who she is talking at.
The stone wall preacher, probably.

What is being Billy Joeled?

I have to go back the way I came and the guy on the corner
is still going.

"If you believe in an inner god
and you can accept death as an end,
whether you fear the end or not,
then there is no need for a religion or a church.
You should know that god is not anywhere else
but within you. And god is not anything else but you.
This is my God."

I say, "Yeah, but my god's better than yours".

More doubt

And I doubt
and I drink
and I smoke
and I'm drunk
and I know
and I don't
More doubt

Unclench

The big fisted, fat fingered doctor of the bum
had another go today.
I don't think he enjoys the fingering,
he might enjoy my discomfort.
It doesn't matter if he finds something or not,
what can they do?
Any option is pretty bad.
Just carry on and hope
for the best, I guess.
It must be time for a walk.

Weary paths

Aware, wary, weary, but not afraid
Weary feet wear weary paths
Small town fears come to pass
Big town reality too far away
Get away from comes with you
Anonymity looks you up in the phone book
You can't hide when they know where you are

Spittle spittle

Spittle spittle, back into the bottle,
as I take another large slug.
I chew it right through, like my dad taught me to…
before he went to the grave that he dug.

Worry worry, there's no need to be sorry,
I live the way that I choose.
If you think you can help me, go on and belt me…
I can't feel it when I'm on the booze.

Money money, it all gets so fuzzy,
I don't know what I do with it all.
But I'm willing to bet, that of all of the people I've met…
I'm always the last one to fall.

Stagger stagger, to a bed where I gather,
the last of my failing wits.
And try to remember what I did on my bender…
fill in the missing bits.

Better better, I'm glad that I met her,
she was the yin in my yang.
She got rid of my heartache, my backache and headache…
and cured me of my over-hang.

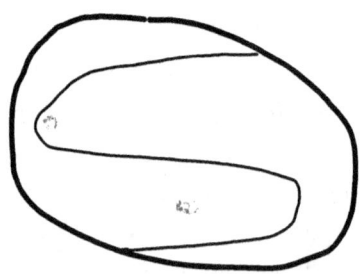

Rose

I sat on my couch waiting for the conversation
that I knew was coming, focus on nothing.
The scrap of paper between books caught my eye
and immediately a memory made its mark.
It was very late and a real effort to retrieve the book
but I lurched across the three metres to grab it from the shelf.
I opened it to a page with a real pressed rose and
the word "Rose" written in large loose texta.
In my mind it completed the perfect puzzle,
I remembered that she'd said – "did you find it?"
And earlier, "it's only one word", smiling.
Flipping through the note book, I found a poem in the spine.

Lust

*Lust may turn into love
Love not into lust?*

*Death without life but not
Life without death?*

*Hate without love but no
Love without hate?*

Linger

The smell of her lingers
though we didn't share a bed.
I breathe deep of day old perfume
and embrace it as it envelops me.
The smell surrounds me with all-pervading pungency
and lowers the image of her down on me.
It torments and it excites
and with cruel intention,
the smell of her lingers.

Loss

When a daughter, in her dying moments pleads, "please, don't leave me", the mother's heart is wrenched out of place.
Out of place, out of time, out of body.
Destroyed.

How long can a loss linger?
Forever and a day.

When a mother, exhausted, says, "I'm going now". And lets go of her life.
Holding hands with her daughter, whose heart is wrenched out of place.
Destroyed.

Out of place, out of time, out of body.

How long can a loss linger?
Forever and a day.

Life and death

Life is all around us
As is death
Life is taken for granted
Death can come as a surprise
Life is expected
Death not so much

W's

The Wailing Wall
Versus the
The Whaling War
On Saturday TV
A choice of a documentary
On Saturday TV
Men kissing walls
(and wailing)
Or men killing fish
(whales or not)

Al

How are ya Al?
Well Tom, I'm dying.
Yeah, of course,
Sorry Al.

Five times
You never find time
You have to make time
Cause at some point in time
Your time is up
No more time

The Mourning

There was devastation
Bernie drove straight into the pole
Ending at Wood Street
They tried but couldn't stop him
From driving
Pissed for sure
Everyone pissed as well
Still they tried to stop him
Pissed off in the morning
And now in mourning

Counting

Counting off the ticking of the clock
Just like the decisions you've made
Until the ticking stops
No more decisions
They are done

Counting off the ticking of the clock
Like the heart beats you've had
Until the beating stops
No more beats
They are done

A long time dead

I don't like the frequently used phrase –
"they died doing something they loved".
Just because; if someone dies doing something they loved doing and it was an ill-timed and unfortunate happening that killed them while they were doing that thing that they loved doing, then it is very possible that they would really like to still be alive to be doing that thing that they love doing.
Not having died doing something they love.

Frame

Even the Buddhists were trying to fuck me up, Pete said.
Picture your life, they said.
Picture your life in a frame.
Imagine the space around your life in the frame, they said.
Now take away your life and imagine what's left.

Mind the

Choice chance circumstance
or
How you got where you are
The choices you have made
The chance that that thing happened
The circumstance or stances you came from
or find yourself in
Choice chance circumstance

Shoes

I should have taken the photo.
I saw it, wanted to stop and take the photo,
but I kept going. Thinking turn back, turn back,
take the photo:

Shoes photo

A stark bus stop, Maiden Gully.
No shelter; baked, rocky, bone-dry.

A pair of faded red shoes.
The type you'd wear to the races,
randomly discarded but
landing symmetrically.

Feet and legs that aren't there.
45 degrees by two feet.
No cover; baked, rocky, dry.
A pair of faded red shoes.

Short life happy

I feel so lucky to be loved
Sometimes guilt makes me feel unworthy
Sometimes cynicism makes me love less
Mostly returned with great gratitude

I feel so old some of the time
In mind with a million stories
In body abused, sick and tired
Wasting away, with or against my will

I feel so young some of the time
In people, youth, child
In awe and laughter and sadness
The connection in happiness and self

I feel so finite all of the time
So quickly it goes and is gone
A billion years stretching out either side
Must make a short life happy

Bad gas

I get home around 9pm, a few people in tow,
the Sunday jam session done.
L is in front of that crappy gas heater,
finishing Saturday's left-over chicken pizza.
Drinks all round and a new pizza is on the way.
Pretty soon, L looks hot in the face
and says, "I don't know how I feel".
Sitting on the toilet we see large red welts over her thighs
and more appearing on her head and torso.
Her body is bubbling inside to out
and she does not feel good.
Drunk anyways I say, "let's go", supporting her through
the house. The peeps are saying "wait". But for what?
We are in the car and out the window it's,
"I'm not waiting, lock the door when you go."
Into the emergency room.
No one else there but the glassed off receptionist who thinks
we are overdosing, maybe violent and is unsure of what to do.
Holding L up, I have to shout through the glass,
"Food poisoning, please get us in."
She does and we're into a cubicle.
L is still bubbling inside, bubbling welts on the outside.
Something is rising, rising.
The lovely Nurse Trinny, working out what's what.
And as we all see the expulsion readying,
Trinny holds up a small stainless-steel dish.
As the vomit goes into it, past it, over and around it
and her, like a small strong pressure hose.
She takes a step back. Even at that distance,
the vomit shoots the dish straight out of her hands
and into the corner, bouncing and spinning with that
steel on hospital floor clanging noise.
Trinny looks at me and then at L in admiration.
Bad chicken, bad gas, super vomit!

Vape

I am in the On ya Clivia version
of the franchise shop selling the vaping device.
I'm deciding on the purchase and the super sales person
is happy to say hey, you get a free set of sunglasses
with every purchase over 44 dollars.
Fantastic I say, getting into the positive vibes.
There is a tall plasticky stand holding all the
15-dollar sunnies.
I grab a pair and the whole thing nearly goes over.
I say to super sales person, wow that nearly went over.
She said yeah, it's really, really wonky.
That is all good, I say, as I keep spinning the thing to look.
I spin it so I'm looking out to Mitchell St and the guy goes,
Hey, you've got more hair than me.
I have a fresh number one cut with a monk bald spot.
He has a 2-foot long white beard and
scraggy long hair to match.
I say, I don't think that that is true
And he says yeah, nah, that is true,
that that is not true.
I say to the super sales person,
I think he might have thought I was some-one else.
She said yeah, it's really, really wonky.
It doesn't matter that she hasn't heard what I said.
I head over to the counter where the super customer service
person is waiting, and say to him, Hey, there's seems to be a
problem with the thing that I bought last time.
He says, yeah, in this case, I think the internet is your best friend.
He is a super customer service person, and all caring and
in all sincerity, he leans in close and gently asks,
Do you have the internet at home?
I laugh, haha ha. And say no, I don't, even though I do.
And he says oh ok, so you don't have a best friend.
So, take this for your other thing with a problem.
And super sales person says, here's your free sunnies,
They look great, she says, but ohh, they're really, really wonky.

The Massage Shop

Room number 4, straight in if you want
Ah I'll just use the loo, if you've got one?
Yeah, yeah, just down the back

Room number 4, strip down to undies,
lay face down with no towel
Cause it's 35 degrees outside and similar inside
Music's going but I can hear the other cubicles
Always the client, only sometimes the massager

Do I put my head in here?
Yes, that's it, keep your undies on,
Face down in there, someone soon

Hello, hello
Yes, I'm Christina

In her 70's at least
What, first time, yes
Yes, the sore spots please
Ohh, you're very strong
No no, it's very good
I'll come to you again oh yes, that's good

Bob, on the other side
Oh yeah, ohhh that's it
Yeah yeah, ohhh
Ohhhh, who am I going to see
when you're away
Oh yeah, can't say, no worries
I'll see ya next week anyway
Yeah ohh yeah, that feels good

Retail woman
Comfortable?
Yes, thank you, oh, my feet and legs
And my hips.
Very busy in retail
All day on my feet on concrete
Pressure…? Very good, yes
What? That's HRT, yes menopause

Female mid-50's
I learnt to say sooksme
Ah, sukmah
Yes, that's it
You know how I said I had no sore spots
Well, that is a sore spot
It hurts but I like it too
I know it's good for me
Ah, sukmah mewali
(I hurt you, you are welcome)

In the foyer is a 60-something
bob-cut female with grand-son
I'm getting more angrier with you
Wait there, don't move
Howdy says the booking bloke
Are you doing the massage
Um no, we have very good massagers for you, not me
Oh ok. You! Sit down there
I'll be back in half an hour

Hayley lay on the table for about eight minutes
Then phones the shop to tell them she's still waiting
Later a technique she has never experienced startles her
With a sharp referred pain in her stomach
I'm from Switzerland she explains

Sounds like a big man asking
Wanting someone to walk on his back
For any sort of feeling at all

Yeah, shopping at Aldi and some weeding...
I walked way too far...
My shoulder is really sore...
I have problems with both arms and both legs...

Music's going, I am stripped bare
35 degrees outside and similar inside
I can hear the other cubicles

Put your head in there, keep your undies on
Someone soon

Kids gone wild.

Brothers, ten and eleven years old.
One on a little dragster bike, no helmet.
The other one running beside.
Running beside, running ahead, running back.
Running, running. And swearing.
Fuck you, dickhead.
And throwing things.
Chips and gravy from Gillies pie shop on the corner,
a lit cigarette, a squashed VB can.
He rides down the one way street, cars stopping, bipping.
The other one running behind. Fuck you dickhead.
Throws the chips and gravy against the shop window.
Fuck you dickhead – the shop owner and the kid saying
the same thing to each other.
Shop owner Daz says fucken little shits.
With a hint of where are you kids from and
understanding them a bit.
Fuck you dickhead, the smaller one yells.
And Daz ducks under the last chips thrown.
Running, running, running.
Running beside, running ahead, running back.
And swearing. Fuck you dickhead.
A woman in the carpark says to another, did they
try to get to you as well?
Oh yeah, he's so small, but the crazy anger, still a bit scary.
He rides straight across the street, the Rolls' driver brakes
quickly to just avoid hitting him and jumps on the horn.
Fuck you dickhead.
They are so young.
One on a little dragster bike, no helmet.
The other one running beside.
Running, running, running. And swearing.
Dickhead. Fuck you.

Letter to band members (former)

Milan Kundera wrote of the photo
of the seven Communist Party leaders,
somewhere cold wearing seven warm furry hats.
Smiling, celebrating good times and being friends.
And then a year later the exact same photo appears,
with seven warm furry hats
but only six Communist Party leaders.
One having been dispatched
for transgressions real or just accused.
But the seven hats remain,
one furry hat just floating in the air behind the
six other hats with people in them.
Physical representation of the ex-member.

And so, from my last gig and party,
there was a fantastic photo of four of the five
long standing musical brothers, arms around shoulders,
very happy about it all.
The photo was used as band promo for a while.
And other than a cymbal or two,
in the bottom right of the photo,
the only gear to be seen is my
23 kilogram Fender Super 60 amp.
The splitter that is me, not in shot.
And the Fender amp is the floating hat,
a fucking heavy one at that.
Physical representation of the member that
is no longer in the group, the party, the band.
Comrades and brothers no more.

Mum's verandah

I am on mum's verandah, very late or very early, drinking way too fast and trying to write a letter. Thinking of our last phone call, I start, Dear So and So,...
Unexpectedly, raindrops fall rhythmically on the house and the trees. To my eyes, tiny globes of light in the lush green plants and leaves glitter in replicas of small galaxies. The air, night and damp, morning and fresh, seems touchable – heavy but so good. It feels like calm and for once, peace. In the letter, I am going to tell the frog story.

Frog story

It was Kailis street, very early in the morning this time, a couple of drinks on the couch and we had seen the frog a bit earlier, hopping in the kitchen. Then we heard the gentle bonk, bonk, bonk on the door out to the stairs on the other side of the house. And I turned to Neil and said – that'll be the frog wanting to go out. So, Neil got up and opened the door to the concrete stairs and the frog back pedalled from behind the door and hopped out. And down the concrete stairs. The frog story.

Bonk

It's funny – bonk, bonk, bonk was the game that dad used to play – gentle headlock and firm knuckles rapping rhythmically on the head. Bonk, bonk, bonk.

Could have been an onomatopoeic frog, a frog called Bonk.

Think

Think. Think. Think. Do; don't think. Think, think, think. Do; not think. Think, think. Do not think. Right? Think then don't think. Think that thought. But don't think about it. Think, think, think. No; don't think! Watch that thought. There it goes. Think it, know it, live it. Think about it...then don't think about it. Think. Think. Think. Do; not think. Think, think, think. Do not think. Think it out.
Think, think, think. Don't think.

Scream

I was really disappointed when I came across the print
in an old pop art book. I thought that the drawing
you had given to me was an original.
You should have told me that it wasn't.

Eggshells

Eggshell fragments fly through the air
As my mind screams out in primal fear

Into the brightness from the blackness beyond
Out of the nothing which is where we come from

Eggshell fragments fly all around
As my dying lungs scream out for air

Back to the blackness and the nothing complete
Back where we came from
To the bright light beyond

K

I think her name was K. I guess she had some issues
that she was working through.
I'm not sure why she ran here – there were places much
closer. Like the cop shop for a start. She seemed scared but
I'm pretty sure nothing had happened.
But 2am, banging on the door, finding her slumped
up against the wall on the verandah.
Yep OK, yes, you're OK. A calming drink and pretty soon
asleep on the couch. Drop her home in the morning and
suggest she seek a little help. Just not from me.

Seventeen

Seventeen, I could not believe,
looking again, I could.
Listening, hearing what I want to
but also your truth.

Explain. I left home at 15.
I listen to people.
A short answer to what question?
Am I deep or wise or are you
a shit-deep pretender?

Silent types, all round good types.
Too tired wasted drained
and too surrounded by people
to talk nice inanities.

Drag us down listening,
listen till we drop.
A thousand stories,
countless sagas
won't leave us alone.

And what now idle thoughts,
digest all you hear?
Try to make sense?
Can't. Too angry at all.

Forced to hear when
you've heard enough
for the long moment
to keep my mind and
stomach churning.

Silence complete.
Listen to myself.
Calming calm.
Agreement doesn't matter.
Just be.

Drink

Drink. Drink. Drink. Do? Don't drink? Drink, drink, drink.
Do; not drink. Drink! Drink! Do not drink. Right? Drink then
don't drink. Watch that draught. But don't drink it.
Drink, drink, drink. No; don't drink! Watch that draught.
There it goes. Drink it, know it, live it.
Drink about it...then don't drink about it.
Drink, drink, drink. Do; not drink. Drink, drink, drink.
Drink it out. Do not drink. Drink, drink, drink. Don't drink.

Rat story

The cat, Buke, was a supreme hunter of other animals.
Which apart from me not liking birds and other animals being
killed also meant I had to kill the biggest rat I had ever seen
with a wooden garden stake. She had herded or dragged it in,
well more than half her size. Not the same as killing a vampire
with a garden stake. Not through the little rat heart with a
wooden stake and tiny hammer. I just used it as a long skinny
club. I got it first time on its head and brain. Which was good
because I didn't want a huge angry and now very bloody rat
going crazy in the kitchen. Buke thought it was still under the
stove so just sat staring in the opposite direction.
I hit it again just to make sure it was dead. It was a big rat.

Buke was also a supreme gatherer of other animals.
Herding birds, lizards, a ferret into the house. A puppy.
How did she do that? The blue heeler pup in the corner single
couch in the lounge room. I am watching through the door
crack. Buke is sitting front on to the chair and the pup.
If the pup moves, Buke swipes with her claws and
the pup sits down. Such control. It continues, pup looks to
move, cat swipes right, pup sits back. I hit the puppy with the
long skinny club. I got it first time on its head. Buke is looking
this time, staring wide eyed.
I didn't hit the blue heeler pup at all.
I asked about and returned it to owners a street away.
Buke is licking herself on the back verandah.

Doing a Huw

Walking winter nights in Bendigo,
down a noiseless, timeless street.
Imagine, waking the sleeping children!
In a street where you walk through a photograph
and the crack of a leaf echoes.
In a place, you are alone, no world exists.
A sound will break the spell, be careful where you step.
Breathe in pure chill night, breathe out frozen air.
Walk the road with no sound and exit,
with nothing at all disturbed.

Sneaking

Sneaking up on corners
dancing with the light
swerve the slippery creek
squeeze through the mist

to surprise your house
on stumbling in its street

Stagger with the footpath
winding on the gutters
bumping into cars
dodging all the way

2 steps forward hop
3 steps back stop
Find the door that's there
fall into the room
Float onto the bed
landing gently
as I should

Very

I jumped up to switch off the light when I heard the footsteps on the verandah. Shuush Vee, keep quiet.
Smack, bang, bang on the wall.
Loud whispered debate of inebriated (very) two.
Thud, thud stomping away. Moments of silence.
Shuush, keep keeping quiet.
Ayy, we got away with it...!
Stomp, stomp, stomp...no we didn't!
Bang, bang, bang on the front door.
Very reluctant, I get up and open it.
Hey you two (very). Where does J live?
I dunno, why? Splutter, splutter, very angry, disrespected, not happy. I'm sure he didn't mean it, don't get angry from it. Here, have a bottle. Awright, thanks. Very angry, disrespected.
Awright, see ya. Yep, drive carefully (very).

Buy

Buy. Buy. Buy. Do; not buy. Buy, buy, buy.
Do; not buy. Buy, Buy. Do not buy. Right? Buy then don't buy.
Watch that buy. But don't buy it.
Buy, buy, buy. No; don't buy. Watch that buy.
There it goes. Buy it, know it, live it.
Buy it...but don't think about it.
Buy, buy, buy. Do; not buy. Buy, buy, buy.
Buy it out. Do not buy. Buy, buy, buy. Don't buy.

Infused coffee

She was young, tattooed and not happy making coffee
at a freeway exit service station early on a Sunday.
Infused by her own very special blend,
the coffee tasted unhappy.

Mind's Eye

She said, "I wrote this song. It's not that good.
I was watching a movie and the intro credits
rolled across a light blue sky background.
It was a bit like the Star Wars intro but less impressive.
It looked nice though so I wrote this song:

My mind's eye opens and sees it all there,
Unfolding perfectly to lay it all bare.
In a 3D panorama encompassing time and space,
stretching out forever in a never ending trace,
to the near and distant future laying there in wait,
for my life to catch up to it and so becomes my fate.
My mind's eye opens. My mind's eye is open.
You play a C-D-Em-G progression.
Like I said, it's not that good."

And I'm looking back and saying, the past should only ever be –
that was what happened. And it informed who we are but that is
not how, what or who we are now.

Music as religion

Music is his religion
He plays at the altar every day
Big rhythmic prayers
That can take an age to learn
Plays out loud better than most
And it can be very very loud
Ask the devotees
re their ears and drums
And it can be so soft
Like a constant whisper to the god
He prays hard most days
Plays hard on the others
And he thinks out loud
Better than anyone he knows
Every day he prays and plays
And prays on his altar
Music is his religion

A small me

I am a small me
A babushka
Mini

But not in a good way
A little me
a lot unhappy

Inside a small me
Layers reveal

A smaller me
More and more
Unhappy

The more and more unhappy
The smaller and smaller I become
A million mini babushkas

Sad babushka sadder and sadder
And smaller and smaller
The sadder you get
The smaller you are

And not in a good way
A little me, a lot unhappy
Tiny mini babushka
A small me

Little Lies

You can tell little lies and you can tell big lies.
You can tell white lies and you can tell black lies.
Or you could lie by saying nothing at all.
You can lie to save yourself or lie to sell yourself.
But you just can't say you tell no lies at all.

One word can cause it:
Saint
Martyr
Liar
Whore

One word can cause it:
Cheat
Bastard
Bitch
That C word that some don't like at all

She said:
I am much better at lust than I am at love.
It is much easier to love a body
than it is to love a person and
toothbrushes are personal,
sex isn't.

Is she a:
Saint
Martyr
Liar
Whore
That C word that some don't like at all

You can tell little lies and you can tell big lies.
You can tell white lies and you can tell black lies.
You can lie to save yourself or lie to sell yourself.
You can lie by saying nothing.
But you just can't say that you tell no lies at all.

He said/she said

He said, "We talk of using people and of being used.
We talk of ill communication and of being abused.
We have only communication and then each other
to use ourselves."

She said, "That's bullshit. Stick with the devil you know.
That is enough. Toothbrushes are personal and sex isn't.
You, man, think differently."

He said, "You are my angel of death, for you I will die.
Not because I want to but because you are it!
An angelic beauty who will bring only blackness and doom."

She said, "Fuck off. Am I not the balance of all things?
Take that shit back."

He said, "OK, I take the bit about blackness and doom back.
And the angel of death bit."

She said, "Thanks. Oh, I used your toothbrush last night."

He said, "Right."

She said, "It's not because I want to get personal. I just needed to clean my teeth."

He said, "But then what? It doesn't make sense that your teeth are clean and that whatever I find or have found, means nothing to you or me."

She said, "<u>That</u> doesn't make any sense. Everything means something. What did you find?"

He said, "Some hairs. That some words can cause blackness and doom. That my toothbrush and sex are the same to you, almost equally."

She said, "Yeah, well. We are right. We can talk, we can not talk, say lots or not much at all. It doesn't matter cause in the end, it's all the same. Confused bullshit, misunderstood non-communication."

He said, "Yep."

Perfect circle

I say what I didn't mean to
You say what you don't mean
We have a lot to talk about
But not very much to say
Choose to say nothing
By way of an answer
Around and around
In a perfect circle
of non-communication

The search for clarity continues

Communication is a wonderful thing
Especially the imaginary kind
Someone said "communication is
in the mind of the audience"
What happens when the only audience is you?

Friendship

Friendships last only while the faults
and the foibles can be accepted

But the assertions of the time of
Forever a mate
Were proven wrong long ago

When comfort was your most important thing
More than friends, more than wife, more than family

But with 10 years of dis-comfort ending your life
Proving all your assertions wrong
And more

I tried to say that a friendship will last
Only while the faults and the foibles are accepted

But you did not want that to be known
Or to know it

And all the dis-comforted years ending your life
Proved all your assertions wrong
And more

Smarter than the rest, mano a mano,
better than them all
Doesn't stop whatever it is that kills you

When comfort was your most important thing
More than friends, more than wife, more than family

Doesn't stop whatever it is that killed you

Unread eulogy

I'm sure a lot of you remember Father Ted, the Irish TV comedy series. Father Dougal was number two priest to Father Ted and was known as not being the smartest priest in the clergy.

In the opening scene of an episode Ted and Dougal were walking the track back to their parochial house on Craggy Island. Returning from a four-day retreat and seminars on all things catholic and being a priest,
Dougal looks and says, "Ted?"
Ted says, "Yes, Dougal."
Dougal says, "Well, you know this god thing."
Ted says, "Yes, Dougal."
Dougal says, "What's all that about then?"

It is, I think, a pretty good question.
What is this god thing all about?

And if you substitute the word life for the word god, then that is also a pretty good question.
This life thing. What's all that about then?

So, mum's life. Pearl's life is why we are here and thinking about what her life was all about.

I think her life was about love. First and foremost.
Love of children, love of nature, love of colour, love of water.

Her life was about a love of giving. To her family, to her friends, her children's friends, the friend's families and their family's friends. To her grandchildren, her grandchildren's friends, the grandchildren's friend's families and…you get the idea. There was a lot of giving throughout her life.
Giving of herself and what ever there was that she had, that could be shared.

I think it was a life, well lived, for a long time.
And we are all left to wonder, just like Dougal did,
this god thing, this life thing….
what's all that about then?

Dwelling

Dwelling on the past
Can't fix the present
Don't live in today
Yesterday was better

Forget the future
It's never what it was
Or what it could be
And tomorrow will be here again
As quick as yesterday went / seems / is
And now continues on and on

Today can affect yesterday
Yesterday fucks tomorrow
Which is already here
Here is already gone
Gone is where it was

Forget the future
It's never what it is
Or what it could be
And tomorrow will be here
and gone again
Think of the future
As it becomes the past

How to save the planet

8 billion people and counting.
How many billion years before us
and how many after?
Thinking of your kids, your grandkids?
50 to 100 years, one hundred and twenty, tops.
Thinking of what?
One thousand years, 10,000 years, a million?

8 billion people and counting.
If we really want to save the planet,
we humans have to become extinct.
When do we do it?
100 years, one thousand years, 10,000 years?
There was a movie, I don't remember the name.
They talked about the earth as an orange.
And humans as the mould, ever multiplying,
forever spreading.
Always destroying and bringing extinction.

Forever?
We can't know forever.
One hundred years, two hundred years,
1,000 years. Now?
When do we humans do it?
To save the planet.

How to save the planet

Earth

'Cause of the earth
'Cause of the dirt
And back to it you go

Letter

She was trying to write a letter, Dear So and So,
Loving a body is easier than loving a being.
I was better at lust which I know you know...
But the phone call got her thinking,
'I like a good resolution, but it doesn't always come.'

If you would like to write to me,
with a question or for a response,
please post to:

Tom
PO Box 866
Bendigo Victoria
Australia   3552

www.ingramcontent.com/pod-product-compliance
Lightning Source LLC
Chambersburg PA
CBHW072109290426
44110CB00014B/1878